The Universe and Human Stupidity

C.M. Ellis

Presentation by *BookLeaf Publishing*

Web: www.bookleafpub.com

E-mail: info@bookleafpub.com

ISBN: 9789394788008

First edition 2022

Again?

Where once I though how ever
Did i manage to pull through?

I signed up for another challenge
To write poems anew!

No sooner had I sent my name,
Inspiration ran away...

And now I have to catch it
In one poem per day...

Coffee Table Book

Sometimes I feel
Like a coffee table book
Culture or nature or photos within
That people use as ornaments
And never look inside

I sit at home
Brimming with stories and facts
Unopened
Like a coffee table book

Silent Witness

O mask
Hanging on my wall

Your sculpted empty sockets
Staring at the world go by

Your eyes will slowly fill with dust
You cannot see the hours fly

Where did you come from? No one can tell.

What have you witnessed? Nobody knows.

O mask
Hanging on my wall
Staring as life goes by...

Journalful of Junk

A scrapbook's too much work
Too much money and crafting supplies

A diary is not for me
A daily entry is too much, don't you agree?

A sketchbook's nice but
Those blank pages mock me to do more

A bullet journal's fun and all
But my fingers would be sore

A journalful of junk instead
Is messy and random and all of the above

It's also the only one that
Has everything I love!

Two More Haikus

I.
From my mind to the
Page is a trajectory
That is infinite

II.
Deer walk the backyard
Squirrels that jump from branch to branch
Nature surrounds me

Reading Weather

Clouds and mist and dull gray skies,
Lazy days they signify.

I settle down with a good book
And plan to stay all day inside.

I get a cocoa cup perhaps,
Or maybe some green tea
Reading weather's nice, don't you agree?

Greatest Fear

I fear the boredom and
Complacency
Of never doing
Something new

No places to visit or
People to meet or
Even
A book to read

I am deathly scared of
Running out
Of things to see
And do

And though it tires me
And takes me by surprise

I do believe
I couldn't do much
Better

At escaping

Boredom's clutches

(After all, I even wrote this book)

One Never Knows

Where trees now grow and rivers run
A battle might have taken place.

The trenches overgrown and filled,
Just hiding from your gaze.

That abandoned bowling alley
Rotting in your neighborhood

Might have served as a filming location
For a legend from Hollywood.

Have you ever stopped and wondered if
That house you drive by all the time,

So unassuming and just like the others,
Might once have been the scene of a crime?

Secondhand

I dug up a vinyl in pretty good shape
With songs from a band that I love.

I found a beautiful hardcover book
One of only three thousand around.

Or an ugly but valuable painting
For two dollars? Yes please!

A colorful tie for pocket change too,
and movies and toys abound.

I love to visit secondhand shops
For all the treasures people drop.

Not all days end in victory,
Sometimes the good stuff is gone.

But searching, after all,
Is half the fun.

Why I Envy Jellyfish

Not a care
In the world

No brain
To worry

Just a current
To drift on

And on...

Summary

(With all due credit to Dorothy Parker)

Comments pain you;
Paid advertising is rank;
Screen brightness strains you;
Poor seating causes cramp.

Scammers aren't lawful;
Spam mail won't give;
Social media is awful;
You might as well live.

Dreamcatcher

Dream about dog frequency, old dog, crazy dog.

Monsters terrorize workers near vale.

Covers thugs in graphite to hide his dirty too.

Windchimes four built into house.

Crazy stalking dead in alcoholic beverages.

Demon of killer mother pretty house.

What the hell were all these dreams about?

Why are they all so diverse ?

Should I go buy a new dreamcatcher

Before I dream of something worse?

Song for Springtime

Springtime brings such happiness
And clearer, brighter skies.

And playful shoots and flowers grow
From plants I thought had died!

Skies of blue and trees of green,
The biting cold retreats.

The chirping birds are out in force
Their melodies so gay!

And pollen blankets everything
And ruins people's day!

Nostalgia

Freshly cooked izote blooms
To start a healthy day

If I want to see the beach
It's just an hour away

A bag of fresh cebada drink
Cold and sweet and pink

Familiar faces always near
How I miss my friends so dear

I am relatively sure
That I could think of more

But those things I miss the most
From my dear El Salvador

Walk

I like to go
On
Walks

And spend some time
Alone
With my thoughts

And feel the sun and breeze
Clean out the cobwebs
Of my
Mind

I always come back
So refreshed

Rain

I sat alone all of today

And through the window saw the gray

That signifies storms overhead

I'm used to it, there is no dread

The thunder rumbles from afar

The clouds have blocked the brightest star

The storm will strike anytime soon

No going out for lunch at noon

The rain at last

Comes falling fast

It strikes the ground

And makes such sound

I did not see much more than that

Though through it all I stared and sat

Walking Along a Body of Water

Little turtle in a pond
Do you know what lies beyond?

Is your world the size and shape
Of your home, the manmade lake?

Little turtle did the birds
Tell you of the world beyond?

Did you ever even care
Or as they spoke you merely yawned?

Behind Closed Doors

Closed doors are almost everywhere.
Where do they lead?
It sure beats me.

Closed doors are something secret.
Are they hiding something
Perhaps you're not meant to see?

Suggested Reading

As if there was A Pearl In Every Oyster
Sitting on the World, full of Pluck and Luck
They had Dinner at Eight so often there
The Algonquin name just stuck.

If the world was Going to Pieces,
Because of some Idiot's Delight
Why, The Good Fellow or The Crazy Fool
Might unleash their pen's full might!

While they've gone to Greener Pastures
Still, I play The Melancholy Lute
And fire a Sunset Gun
As their genius I salute.

Life Goes On

I walked around my town today
And settled down in the park
Beneath the solemn statue
Of someone who made their mark.

Who then is he, I wonder?
Immortalized as art!
The plaque is old and dirty,
His features I can barely tell apart.

How many fancy statues are there,
In streets and parks all over the world?

People once honored, now ignored,
Except by pigeons, wings unfurled?

Curtain Call

The time has come the poet says
To talk of may things

Of stars and squirrels and melted glass
Of... wait... isn't the book over?

It is! It is over!

Oh well, mustn't keep you much longer...

The time has come, the poet thinks
To end this little book

He hopes that you've enjoyed it
And will take another look,

He also wants to thank you for putting up with him
And all the crazy poems that were written on a whim.

He wishes it's been just as fun
To read as it was to write!

(Except the the last minute edits in the middle of
the night)